The Crafter's Design Li...

Christmas

Sharon Bennett

David & Charles

This one's for you, Mum x

A DAVID & CHARLES BOOK

First published in the UK in 2004

Distributed in North America
by F&W Publications, Inc.
4700 E. Galbraith Rd.
Cincinnati, OH 45236
1-800-289-0963

Text and artwork Copyright © Sharon Bennett 2004

ISBN 0 7153 1748 2 hardback
ISBN 0 7153 1749 0 paperback

Printed in Singapore by KHL
for David & Charles
Brunel House, Newton Abbot, Devon

commissioning editor Fiona Eaton
desk editor Jennifer Proverbs
senior designer Lisa Forrester
production controller Jennifer Campbell
photographer Karl Adamson

Visit our website at www.davidandcharles.co.uk

David & Charles books are available from all good bookshops; alternatively you can contact our
Orderline on (0)1626 334555 or write to us at FREEPOST EX2 110, David & Charles Direct,
Newton Abbot, TQ12 4ZZ (no stamp required UK mainland).

The author and publisher have made every effort to ensure that all the instructions in this book
are accurate and safe, and therefore cannot accept liability for any resulting injury, damage or
loss to persons or property however it may arise.

contents

the essential techniques

the templates

Introducing Christmas art

Christmas is a time when family and friends come together, a time of giving and thinking of others. But it can also be a time for contemplation and hopefully an opportunity to give time to oneself. Crafts come into their own during this period. Making things for others provides quiet time when we can focus our minds on the people we are making each item for and gain immense creative satisfaction at the same time. In this age of commercialism, a homemade gift is likely to be treasured far more than anything that can be bought in the shops. But don't forget yourself at this time too, and make items for your own home, to be hung on the tree each year and passed down to future generations.

This book is aimed at everyone who is creative and enjoys crafting and who needs a source of inspiring images to work with. It features a host of Christmas motifs to fire the imagination plus an informative guide to help you make the most of the motifs. You'll find plenty of practical hints and tips on how to use the templates to achieve really eye-catching results. Whether you are looking for a motif to suit a particular project or want to find an image to inspire your work, this book has all the answers.

To spur your imagination, take a look at Ideas for Christmas Crafting (page 6), which runs through some popular techniques and explains how to use the templates in this book in different ways. Then turn to Applying Motifs to Craft Media (pages 8–13) to find out how to transfer a template to your chosen project, with helpful tips for achieving the right results. If the image needs some adjustment, refer to Adapting and Combining Designs (pages 14–15), which utilizes designs from the second part of the book, and for some festive glitter and sparkle see Colour and Embellishment (pages 16–19). Finally, see the Project Gallery (pages 20–25), which showcases some of the Christmas templates applied in various ways for the ultimate in inspiration.

If you don't want to bother with the technical details, turn straight to page 26 to find the templates, a fun collection of black-and-white, hand-drawn line images, which cover many much-loved themes from Christmas decorations and foliage to toys and classic nativity scenes, plus invaluable borders and lettering. The images are divided into eight chapters, each beginning with simple designs and progressing to more detailed and intricate imagery. This will help the novice gain in confidence, while providing challenging material for the more experienced crafter. All in all, you'll find this a varied library providing for all your crafting needs.

The colour images here and elsewhere were created using the templates from page 26 onward. Cerne relief adds sparkle to the parcels, left, and richness to the scene opposite page 1 (templates on pages 40 and 90). Glitter perfects Santa, right, (page 31) and bold colour embellishes the tree, top right (page 60).

Ideas for Christmas crafting

There are countless crafts that are ideal for creating and embellishing festive decorations, presents, gift wrapping, tags and greetings cards. For more details about how to make the projects shown here, see pages 20–25.

Metal/foil

Embossing onto brightly coloured foil or metal sheets is a great technique for making cards and personalized gift tags (see page 25). These also look good hung on the tree. Try working sometimes from the back for a raised line and sometimes from the right side for a depressed effect. A touch of paint or a dab of glitter on foil also produces fantastic results.

Stencils

Stencilling is a good technique for producing fast, effective images that can be repeated (see Starburst Gift Wrap, page 25).

Paper

Cutting and tearing images from foil, handmade paper or tissue is highly effective for card making. Combine a number of images and different paper textures to create a variety of Christmas crafts (see Shimmering Surprise Cracker, page 23).

Candle art

Create a truly festive atmosphere by adding Christmas images cut from thin sheets of wax to candles. If desired, combine with candle paints or pens (see page 24).

Modelling

Use the templates to produce three-dimensional or flat models. Both types make excellent tree decorations or can be set in foliage for table centrepieces. Simple designs can also be used for biscuits and cake decorations.

Silk painting

Christmas images painted onto silk can be applied to cards or extravagant covers for small gift boxes, or made into luxurious cushions and scarves. The simplest designs can look beautiful.

Other fabrics

Fabric paints add a temporary or permanent Christmas look to table linen, furnishings or clothes (see Celebration Mistletoe Napkins, page 23). There are many different fabric paints and methods of application: pipe on outliners; stipple on paints for backgrounds; use spray with stencils; apply wax resist; or use puff paint, for example.

Embroidery

Embroider the designs in a colourful variety of glittery threads and use several stitches for texture. For details on transferring a design to cross stitch fabric, see page 13.

Découpage

Christmas papers and photocopied motifs from this book can be combined with basic motifs such as bows, hearts, stars and leaves for a festive feel.

Painting

Paint seasonal images onto a variety of different surfaces such as wood, metal or card. You can even paint over existing images on a tin or gift box (see Winter Wonderland Hatbox, page 20).

Glass painting

Glass is particularly appropriate for Christmas decorations, especially if combined with a metallic outliner. Techniques for background colour like stippling, colour washing or sponging provide added interest. Look for matt, frosted and transparent paints and use them together for exciting effects.

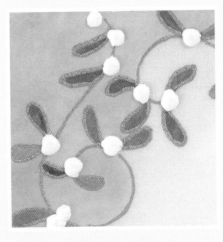

Applying motifs to craft media

The techniques best suited to applying your selected motif to a particular medium depend on the surface. The following pages offer some simple advice on how to do this for the most popular craft media. Guidance is also given on how to enlarge or reduce the motif to suit your requirements (below) and how to create a stencil (page 13).

Enlarging and reducing a motif

Here are three ways to change the size of a motif to suit your project: the traditional method using a grid, or the modern alternatives of a photocopier or scanner.

Using a grid

The traditional method of enlargement involves using a grid. To begin, use low-tack masking tape to secure tracing paper over the original design. Draw a square or rectangle onto the tracing paper, enclosing the image (see below). Use a ruler to divide up the square or rectangle into rows of equally spaced vertical and horizontal lines. Complex designs should have lines about 1cm (⅜in) apart; simpler ones can have lines 4cm (1½in) apart.

Now draw a square or rectangle to match your required design size, and draw a grid to correspond with the one you have just drawn over the image, as shown below. You can now begin to re-create the original image by redrawing it, square by square, at the required scale.

Using a photocopier

For fast and accurate results, use a photocopier to enlarge or reduce a motif. To do this, you need to calculate your enlargement percentage. First measure the width of the image you want to end up with. Here, the motif needs to be enlarged to 135mm (5¼in). Then measure the width of the original motif, which in this case is 90mm (3½in). Divide the first measurement by the second to find the percentage by which you need to enlarge the motif, in this instance 150%. (An enlargement must always be more than 100% and a reduction less than 100%).

To photocopy an image onto tracing paper, use tracing paper that is at least 90gsm. When photocopying an image from tracing paper, place the tracing paper onto the glass, and then lay a sheet of white paper on top of it. This will help to produce a sharp copy.

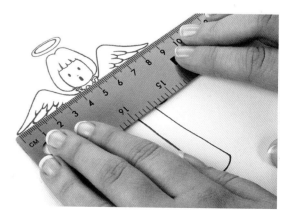

Transferring a motif onto paper, card, wood or fabric

A light box makes it easy to trace an image directly onto a piece of paper, thin card or fabric, but if you don't have one it is easy to improvize with household items. Balance a piece of clear plastic across two piles of books or furniture, and place a table lamp underneath. Place your motif on the plastic and your paper, thin card or fabric on top.

Using a scanner

A third way to enlarge or reduce a motif is to scan the original image on a flatbed scanner or to photograph it with a digital camera. Once the image is on your computer you can either adjust the size using image manipulation software, or simply alter the percentage of your printout size. If the finished result is larger than the printer's capacity, some software will allow you to tile the image over several sheets of paper, which can then be joined together to form the whole image.

An image manipulation package may also allow you to alter the proportions of a motif, making it wider or narrower, for example. Take care not to distort it beyond recognition, though. Once you are happy with your image, it can be saved to be used again and again.

To transfer a design onto wood, thick card or foam, trace the design onto tracing paper using a sharp pencil. Turn the tracing over and redraw on the wrong side with a soft lead pencil. Now turn the tracing over again and use masking tape to secure it right side up onto your chosen surface. Carefully redraw the image – press firmly enough to transfer the motif, but take care not to damage the surface.

Transferring a motif onto foil

To emboss foil, simply take the original tracing and secure it to the foil surface. Rest the foil on kitchen paper. Use an embossing tool or an old ballpoint pen that has run out of ink to press down on the tracing, embossing the metal below. Use the same technique on the back of the foil to produce a raised effect.

Transferring a motif onto mirror and ceramic

Trace the motif onto tracing paper, then turn the tracing over and redraw on the wrong side using a chinagraph pencil. A chinagraph produces a waxy line that adheres well to shiny surfaces, which makes it ideal for transferring designs to coloured glass, mirrored glass and ceramic. Chinagraphs are prone to blunt quickly, but it doesn't matter if the lines are thick and heavy at this stage. Use masking tape to secure the tracing right side up onto the surface. Carefully redraw with a sharp pencil to transfer the image.

Tracing a motif onto glass and acetate

Roughly cut out the motif and tape it to the underside of the acetate or glass with masking tape. It is helpful to rest glassware on a few sheets of kitchen towel for protection and to stop curved objects from rolling. The image will now show through the clear surface, and you can simply trace along the lines with glass outliner or paint directly onto the surface.

If you want to transfer an image onto opaque glass, or onto a container that is difficult to slip a motif behind, such as a bottle with a narrow neck, follow the instructions on page 9 for transferring a motif onto mirror or ceramic.

Transferring a motif onto curved items

Motifs can be transferred onto rounded items, but will need to be adapted to fit the curves. First trace the motif, redrawing it on the underside (use a chinagraph pencil if the container is ceramic). Make cuts in the template from the edge towards the centre. Lay the motif against the surface so that the cuts slightly overlap or spread open, depending on whether the surface is concave or convex. Tape the motif in place with masking tape and transfer the design as before.

Making a template for a straight-sided container

If you wish to apply a continuous motif such as a border to a straight-sided container, make a template of the container first. To do this, slip a piece of tracing paper into a transparent glass container or around an opaque glass or ceramic container. Lay the paper smoothly against the surface and tape in place with masking tape. Mark the upper edge of the container with a pencil. Now mark the position of the overlapping ends of the paper or mark each side of the handle on a mug, cup or jug.

Remove the tracing and join the overlap marks, if you have made these. Measure down from the upper edge and mark the upper limit of the band on the template. Cut out the template and slip it into or around the container again to check the fit. Transfer your chosen template onto the tracing paper, then onto the container.

Making a template for a plate

1 Cut a square of tracing paper slightly larger than the diameter of the plate. Make a straight cut from one edge to the centre of the paper. Place the paper centrally on the plate or saucer and tape one cut edge across the rim. Roughly cut out a circle from the centre of the paper to help it lie flat. Smooth the paper around the rim and tape in place, overlapping the cut edges. Mark the position of the overlap on the paper.

2 Turn the plate over and draw around the circumference onto the underside of the tracing paper. Remove the paper, then measure the depth of the plate rim and mark it on the paper by measuring in from the circumference. Join the marks with a curved line.

Transferring a motif onto fabric

If fabric is lightweight and pale in colour, it may be possible to trace the motif as it is. If the fabric is dark or thick, it may help to use a light box. Place the motif under the fabric on the surface of the light box (see page 9 for information on constructing a home light box). As the light shines up through the motif and fabric you should be able to see and design lines, ready for tracing.

Alternatively, place a piece of dressmaker's carbon paper face down on the fabric and tape the motif on top with masking tape. Trace the design with a sharp pencil to transfer it onto the fabric as shown below. The marks made by the carbon are easily wiped away.

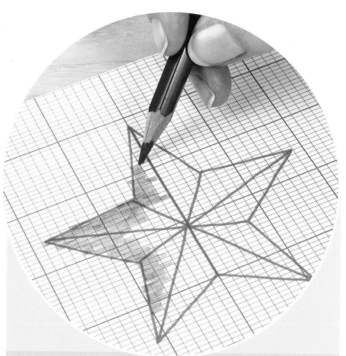

Transferring a motif onto a knitting chart

Use knitting-chart paper rather than ordinary graph paper to chart a knitting design. (Knitted stitches are wider than they are tall and knitting chart paper is sized accordingly.) Transfer the motif straight onto the knitting graph paper (see page 9 for advice on transferring onto paper). Each square on the graph paper represents a stitch. Make sure that you are happy with the number of squares in the motif, as this dictates the number of stitches in your design, and ultimately the design size. Fill in the applicable squares on the chart using appropriate coloured pens or pencils.

Use the finished chart in conjunction with a knitting pattern. Read the chart from right to left for a knit row and from left to right for a purl row. The motif can also be worked on a ready-knitted item with Swiss darning.

Transferring a motif onto needlepoint canvas and cross stitch fabric

Designs on needlepoint canvas and cross stitch fabric can be worked either by referring to the design on a chart, or by transferring the image to the material and stitching over it.

To transfer the motif onto a chart

Transfer the motif straight onto graph paper (see page 9 for advice on transferring onto paper). Each square on the graph paper represents a square of canvas mesh or Aida cross stitch fabric. Colour in the squares that the motif lines cross with coloured pencils or pens. You may want to make half stitches where the motif outline runs through a box. Mark the centre of the design along a vertical and horizontal line (see right) and mark the centre of the fabric lengthways and widthways with tacking stitches.

To transfer the motif directly onto canvas or fabric

With an open-weave canvas or pale fabric it is possible to trace the design directly onto the canvas or fabric. First, mark a small cross centrally on the motif and on the material. On a lightbox (see page 9), place the material on

top of the motif, aligning the crosses. Tape in position and trace the image with a waterproof pen. Alternatively, use dressmaker's carbon paper as explained in transferring a motif onto fabric, opposite.

Making a stencil

Tape a piece of tracing paper over the motif to be adapted into a stencil. Redraw the image, thickening the lines and creating 'bridges' between the sections to be cut out. You may find it helpful to shade in the areas to be cut out. Lay a piece of carbon paper, ink side down, on a stencil sheet, place the tracing on top, right side up, and tape in place. Redraw the design to transfer it to the stencil sheet. Finally, lay the stencil sheet on a cutting mat and carefully cut out the stencil with a craft knife, always drawing the sharp edge of the blade away from you.

Adapting and combining designs

You may be lucky enough to find a template in this book that is exactly how you want it, but if not, the designs can easily be adapted – it's simple and fun and will bring out all your creativity. You'll find that sometimes even subtle changes alter a motif dramatically. Here are a few ideas to get you started.

Simplifying an image

The easiest way to simplify a design is to use the outline of the template to create a silhouette. However, just removing some of the detail from the image can make a simpler motif. Without its embellishments, the decorative bell (see page 53) provides an easy-to-use outline for all types of crafts.

tip

Keep things simple but bright by adding block colour either inside the bell or as a backround to the image.

Adapting an image

A template can be easily adapted to create a completely different look to suit your crafting needs. Here a round parcel (see page 40) has been changed into a square, and the ribbon turned clockwise to give a new design – simple but very effective.

tip

Enlarge a motif if you want to add more detail. For example, a pattern could be added to the gift wrap and ribbon.

Combining images

tip

With practise you can start to combine details from different templates to create unusual and unique images. Play around and experiment with images to get the right end result.

Experiment with combining templates to create a unique image. This cherub (page 88) was flipped to make a pair to place either side of a scroll (page 116) – the cherubs now appear to be holding it. Reversing (flipping) an image is also ideal if you want to create corners to contain a design.

Creating new looks

If a motif appeals but doesn't exactly suit the project idea, all you need is a little imagination to create the image you need. This window (page 81) shows a snowy scene beyond, but just by changing those squares to contain an indoor scene such as a Christmas tree or fireside and then piling snow on the windowsill, you can create a whole new look.

tip

Trace the empty window onto clear film (acetate) and place over another image or message – this is a great technique for handmade cards.

Simple repetition

Repetition produces great results and just one little bit of a design, when repeated, can make an excellent border or frame. Use one simple motif repeated several times, or join repeats together to create a continuous border as shown below (see page 111).

tip

Work out the measurements of the border and roughly calculate how many repeats of the image you will need along each edge before you begin.

Colour and embellishment

Watch these images burst into life with the addition of colour and a sprinkle of glitter or a dab of silver or gold. Traditional Christmas colours like red and green are always popular but seasonal crafting certainly offers the opportunity to experiment and create with an array of colours, textures, sparkle and shine. There are many different products available suitable for all sorts of crafts. Exploring the many options will be fun and rewarding.

Simple outlining

A simple choice, but one that will make a big difference to the look of illustrative work, is to decide if you want an outline around images you are planning to colour. If you choose to include the outline remember that it doesn't have to be black – with paints, try using a thin outline in brown for a more subtle effect. (See page 32 for this image.)

Silhouettes

Simple one-colour line images or silhouettes look good on a bright background. Graduated coloured backgrounds like the one shown are quick and easy to do or simply outline in one colour on a different colour – red on gold for example. (See page 58 for this template.)

tip
Watercolour pencils are an easy way to add colour. Use like crayons then brush with water to blend.

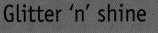

tip

Gently rub foil leaf over a size (glue). It looks great on cards and paper but also on three-dimensional objects.

Glitter 'n' shine

Christmas crafting involves plenty of glitz, with sparkles, glitter and foil – it really is a necessary feature. You can quite literally transform things by adding a splash of gold or silver and a simple metallic border. A touch of gold leaf on this festive bow (page 57) really expresses the Christmas spirit.

Subtle effects

Iridescent paints create a soft but eye-catching result. They are very subtle and rely on the light to reveal just how wonderful they are. Place items decorated with iridescent paints alongside Christmas tree lights to see them come alive. They are available in a range of pretty shades in oils, acrylics, crayons and other mediums. (This template is on page 47.)

Bold colour

Bold areas of colour can be very striking but you may not want large areas of flat colour. To inject more life into painted motifs, try varying the thickness of the paint, stipple into it with a stencil brush or blot it off for a velvety texture. (For this reindeer motif, see page 29.) Try combining paint with pens and add selective areas of glitter with metallic pens or sprays – the tree below (see page 38) shows how effective even a little sparkle can be.

Decorative touches

Colour and texture come into their own when creating seasonal crafts. There are many different products with many different methods of application and this is the one time of the year when it is hard to over-gild the lily. Combining colours and embellishments can create some beautiful results, especially on lettering (see pages 118–119).

tip

When using an image with an added decoration, like these ivy-twined initials, you can add colour to the letter itself or to the embellishment. Experiment with both options to see how you create positive and negative images.

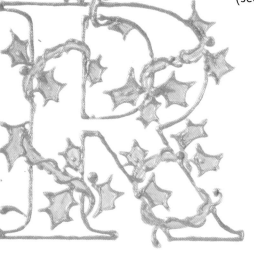

Relief finishes

Cerne relief is sometimes referred to as outliner. It is piped on from a small tube that has a fine nozzle and produces a raised line that dries quite hard, as shown on the candle image, right (see page 59). The result gives a fantastic feel to a design, with an embossed quality that looks sumptuous. However, note that relief paints do require quite a bit of drying time.

tip
Use a special paint and bake outliner on glass for hardwearing results. Fabric outliner is referred to as a 'gutta', and cerne relief is perfect for paper.

tip
Heated glue and foil produces fantastic results using simple images and handwriting – perfect for personalizing items such as cards and tags.

Glitter glue

There are many glitter glues available. Some have a raised appearance and a shiny finish when dry, with others the base liquid disappears as it dries, which creates a just-touched look (powders would have the same effect). For this bauble (page 53), a special glitter glue was applied to paper. Coloured foil was then placed over the top and warm air applied. When the foil was peeled away from the paper, a layer of foil adhered to the glue outline.

   With this technique you can use both the resulting embellished paper (near right) and the remaining foil (far right) – two for one.

Project gallery

Here are some super examples of how simple templates can be transformed into glittering craft creations. Be it gifts or gift wrap, decorations or seasonal table linen, there are countless ways to create beautiful items with the festive motifs in this book. Let these colourful ideas feed your imagination and inspire your own unique craft designs.

winter wonderland hatbox

A beautiful gift box or a gift in itself, here the snowmen from pages 42 and 43 combine with a wonderfully seasonal rooftop scene from page 79 to create a stunning design for this special hatbox. Acrylic paints were used over a white gesso primer then finished with a craft varnish for durability.

bubbly baubles

These bright and cheerful baubles use four simple designs combined with one of the classic snowflake motifs on page 44. The Santa from page 30, a fairy angel from page 46, the donkey from page 71 and an angel from page 88 all make bold and striking images when applied to clear glass baubles using glass paints with frosted and clear cerne relief.

festive platter

A lavish and highly decorative effect was achieved here by positioning the wreath motif from page 69 in the centre of this plate. The edge is decorated with the bow and sash from page 111, while a section of the square parcel from the wreath has been interspersed with the bow and sash edging to mark the four corners. Colour was added with paint-and-bake paints, which are hard-wearing and completely washable. Choose colours that coordinate with your own décor or table colours.

poinsettia candles

The poinsettia motif from page 66 has been transferred to a cream church candle and decorated with candle paints to make this festive table decoration. The gold dots in the centre of the design were cut from shiny gold wax sheet that, once cut, simply peels off and can be pressed in place.

goodwill lantern

A plain hanging lantern becomes a colourful decoration that celebrates the Christmas message of Peace on Earth. The lantern frame has been painted with purple metal paint and the glass panels adorned with various nativity images. The large glass panels alternate a dove from page 103 placed above a border of holly from page 111 with a stained-glass nativity image from page 87. The small glass panels at the bottom of the lantern show a silhouette stable scene from page 96. Glass paints were used in clear and frosted finishes, embellished in places with gold glitter glue.

celebration mistletoe napkins

For those special celebration meals these super napkins will certainly set the scene. The simple mistletoe design from page 111 was traced onto plain cream napkins before being outlined with cerne relief and coloured in using fabric paints. A gold fabric spray that washes out was added for extra sparkle and puff paints, which swell when ironed on the reverse, were used for the mistletoe berries. The partridge in the pear tree is given on page 104.

frosted snowflake glasses

These stylish wine glasses were made by cutting a film stencil using a snowflake motif from page 45 and then spraying through it with glass frosting spray. Either the snowflake can be frosted, or the area around it – by using the snowflake image removed from the centre of the stencil as a mask.

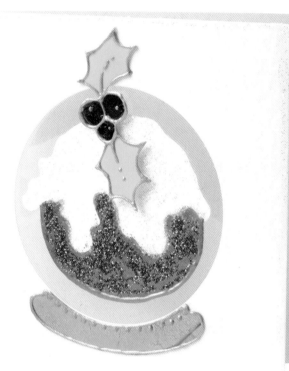

glittering pudding card

Send a jolly season's greeting with this eye-catching card. The Christmas pudding template from page 48 was cut from gold foil and applied to clear acetate, which was then positioned behind the round aperture of a card blank. Gold glitter embellishes the bottom of the pudding and the 'sauce' was created from ultrafine glitter. The holly leaves and berries were outlined on green paper with gold cerne relief and then cut out and glued in place.

shimmering surprise cracker

Crown motifs from page 92 were cut out of red and gold foil and arranged over the length of this jolly cracker. The end sections are decorated with a bead and star border from page 51 that has been piped in gold. A robin (page 102) takes centre stage.

starburst gift wrap and foil tags

The simple star template from page 93 makes an
excellent stencil that can be painted onto coloured
papers to make fabulous gift wrap. The same idea
can be applied to homemade or shop-bought gift
bags and packaging. As a finishing touch add
foil gift tags embossed with a suitable design
such as an initial (pages 118–119), holly leaves
(page 65) or a pretty fairy (page 46).

the
templates

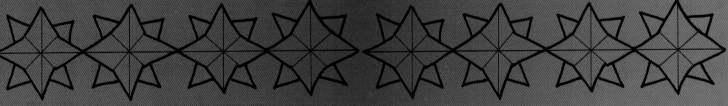

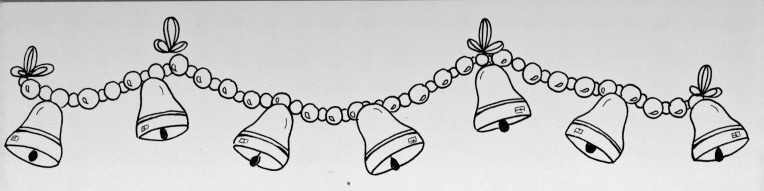

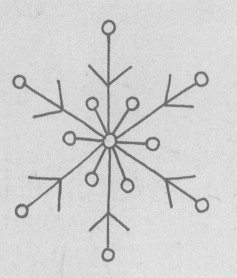

Traditional

Some of the traditions we associate with Christmas date back thousands of years – gift giving, decorating the home with greenery, singing and feasting were all part of Roman and pagan mid-winter festivals celebrated long before the birth of Christ. The familiar figure of Santa Claus was originally based on Saint Nicholas, patron saint of children, but the image we all know and love of a portly Santa clad in red and white riding his sleigh to deliver presents to children was first conceived by the American author Washington Irving in 1809 and crystallized in the drawing of the American cartoonist Thomas Nast in the 1860s. Today, Christmas would not be Christmas without him, so this section has many versions to choose from, along with his reindeer, elves and other traditional motifs such as snowflakes and snowmen, Christmas trees, presents and angels, not to mention festive fare such as turkey and Christmas pudding.

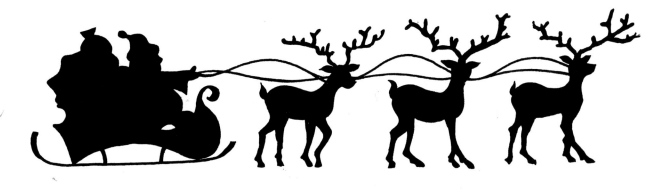

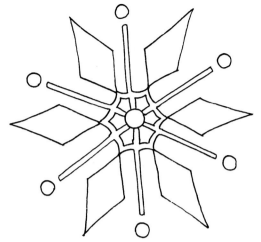

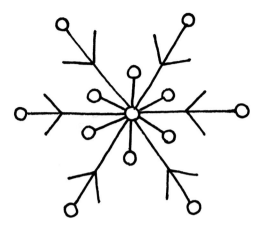

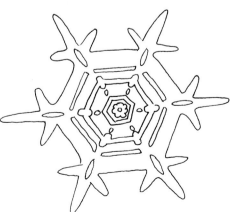

Decorations

Festive decorations are very much a part of Christmas as we know it today, and have a major role in the celebrations. The Christmas tree (see pages 38–39) is often the focus, and is hung with baubles, beads, lanterns, bells, bows and edibles such as gingerbreads, shortbreads, sweets and chocolates. Many of these motifs are included here.

The traditional decorated tree probably developed in Germany, first appearing in a medieval Christmas play about Adam and Eve. By the 1600s many German families were decorating evergreen trees with fruits, nuts, lighted candles and paper roses, and Queen Victoria's German husband, Prince Albert, is thought to have taken the idea to Britain. Now it is a worldwide phenomenon – many capital cities sport towering trees adorned with bright lights to symbolize the festive season.

The decorations here can be used together with a tree motif or combined with other templates in this book. Use metallic or bright colours, especially traditional green and red. (Green represents continuing life during the winter months and the Christian belief in eternal life through Jesus Christ; red symbolizes the blood of Christ shed at the crucifixion.)

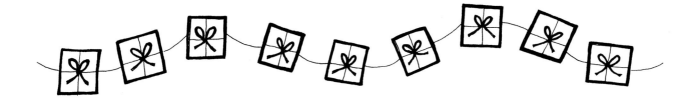

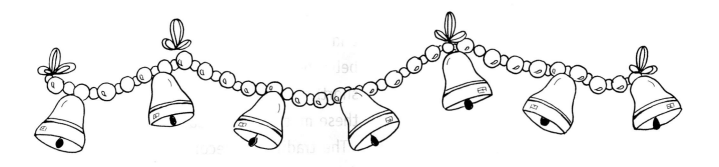

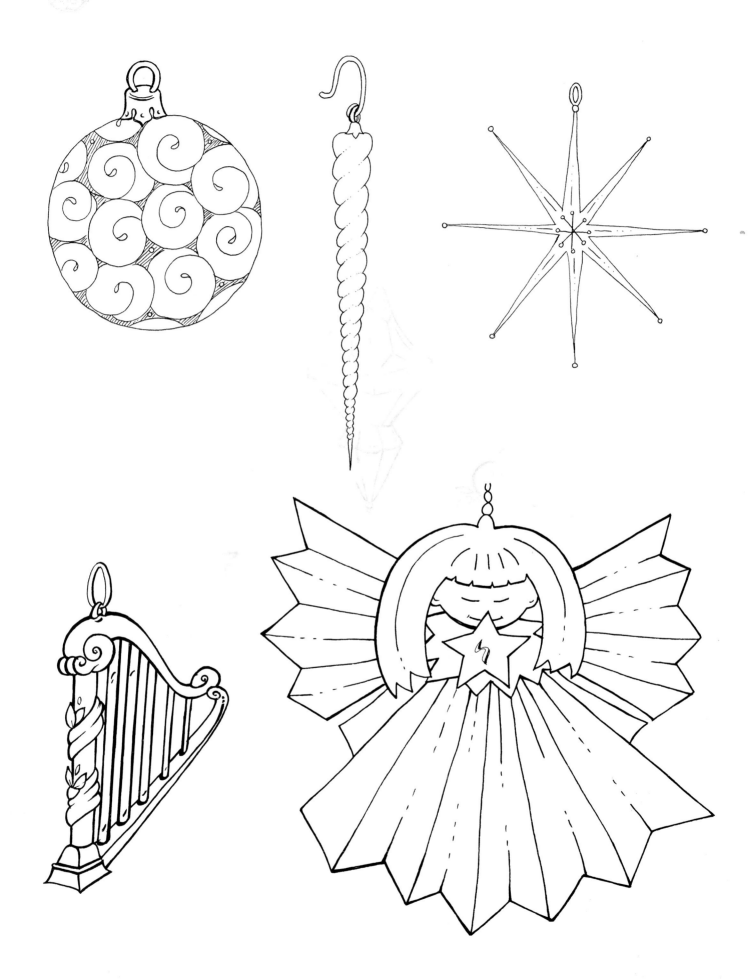

Foliage

Greenery has long been used as a symbol of continuing life during the long winter days when the sun all but disappears. Romans exchanged holly and ivy during Saturnalia and introduced the idea of using wreaths as a sign of victory or celebration. Today's Christmas wreaths are generally based on evergreens and can include other items such as bows, dried fruits and cinnamon bundles. There are a number of wreaths to choose from in this section.

Among the foliage holly and mistletoe are particular favourites. The early Christians called holly the holy tree because its pointed leaves resembled the crown of thorns Christ wore and the red berries symbolize His blood. Mistletoe was considered a powerful plant by the early Celtic people who used it for charms, and today a sprig of mistletoe can be used to claim a Christmas kiss. There are plenty of holly and mistletoe images here, along with other leafy motifs.

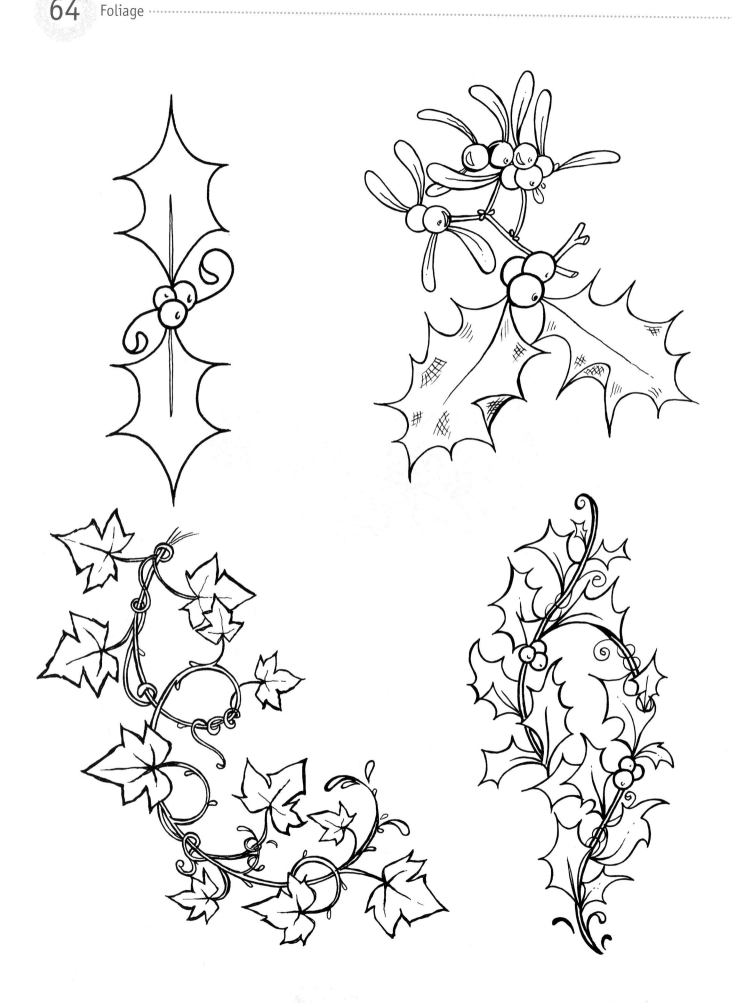

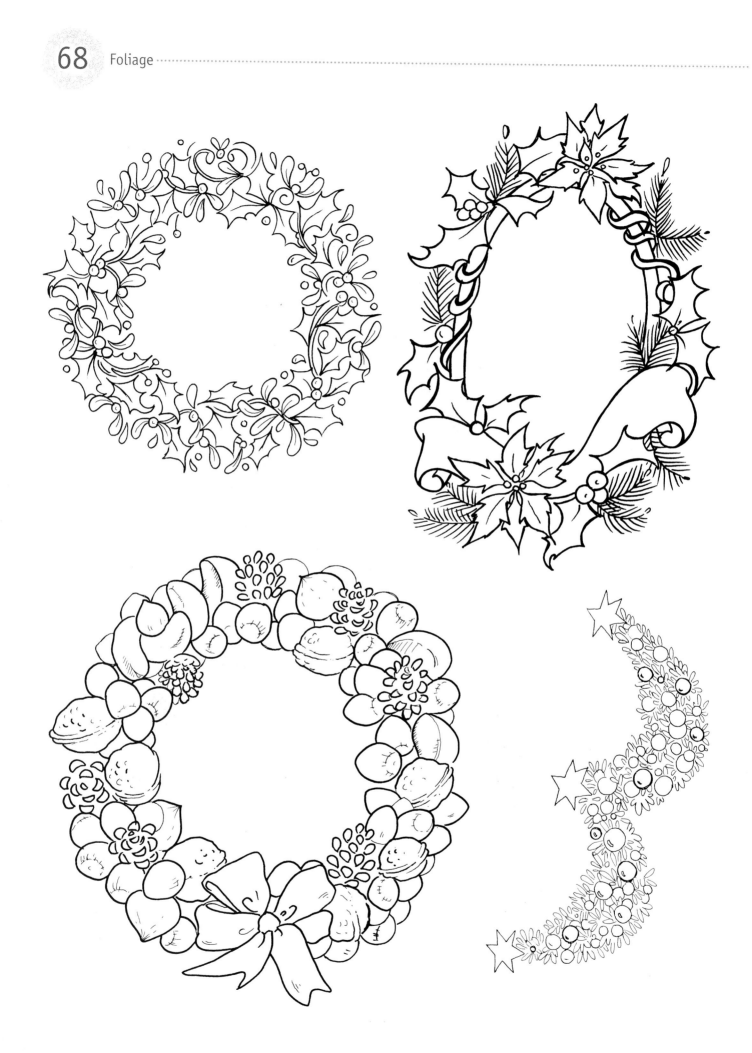

Toys

Exchanging gifts has become a huge part of Christmas, and carries on from the traditions of pre-Christian mid-winter celebrations.

Saint Nicholas was an early Christian bishop who died in the 300s, and became celebrated as the patron saint of children. It is said that Nicholas befriended a nobleman who had three daughters. The nobleman would not provide dowries for his daughters and because of this they could not marry. Nicholas is said to have thrown three bags of money through an open window of the nobleman's house, thus enabling the girls to marry. His association with the bringing of gifts may have evolved from this story.

In many countries Saint Nicholas has been replaced by a non-religious figure, such as Father Christmas, who delivers gifts. Around the world there are many different traditions, with gifts arriving as early as 6th December and as late as 6th January. Children are the main focus of the festivities, so toys are an important element. Traditional versions (see pages 74–77) are particular favourites with grown-ups.

Scenes

Although December may fall at the height of summer for some people around the world, traditional Christmas scenes are linked with snowy hills, sledging and flickering firesides, as shown on the following pages. Most people live in bustling cities today, yet images of sleepy villages with snow-laden rooftops and small groups of carolers huddled around a single lantern are still the most popular at this time of year.

Classic seasonal scenes often appear to represent snippets of a child's memory: gatherings around a real fire; the excitement of bedtime on Christmas Eve; hanging up a stocking or playing in the freshly fallen snow. These are the Christmas scenes we most cherish.

Nativity

No one knows for sure the exact day of Christ's birth, but most Christians celebrate on 25th December. In many churches and homes a nativity scene is displayed in the run-up to Christmas and during the celebrations. Nativity scenes may include Mary travelling on a donkey accompanied by Joseph, the stable where the baby Jesus was born and laid in a manger, the angel appearing to the shepherds and bringing the glad tidings and the three wise men or Magi who followed a star to find the Christ child, carrying gifts of gold, frankincense and myrrh.

Music and song are part of the Christian celebrations as well, and many carols are sung at this time of year. With this in mind, the images here include scenes around the manger, the three kings and their crowns, the star that showed the way, the shepherds and their sheep, angels and choristers with music and instruments.

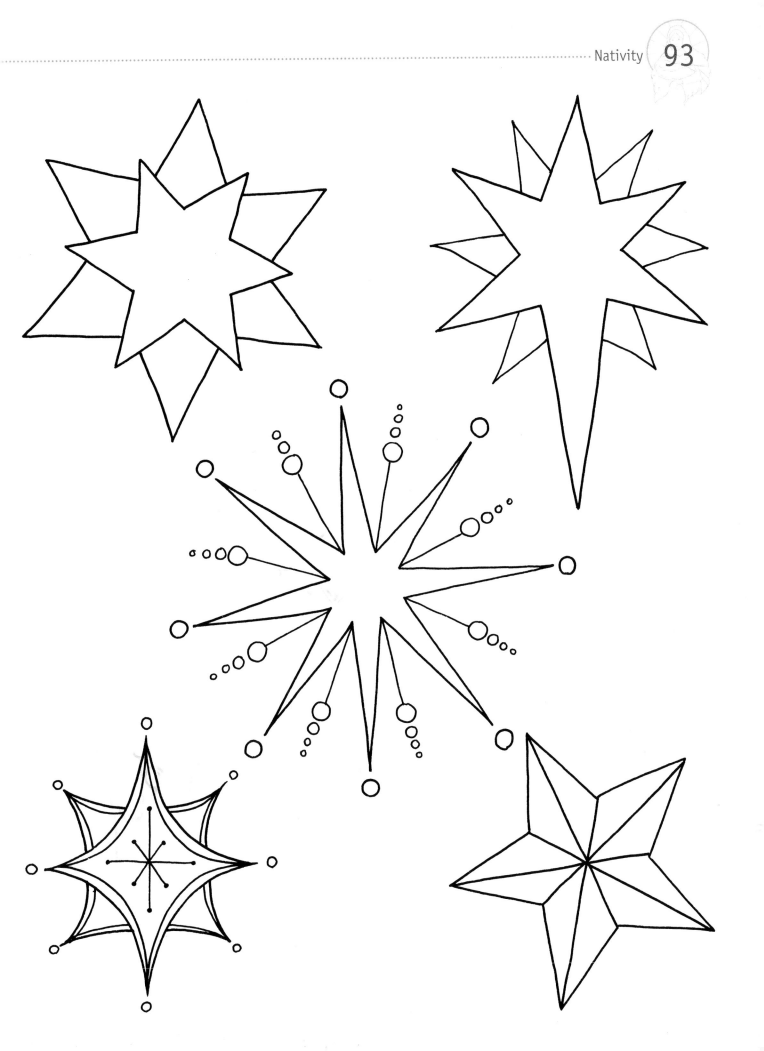

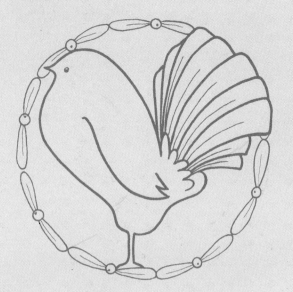

Animals

Certain animals and birds are associated with Christmas and are popularly used as motifs during the festive season. The cheerful robin redbreast, the white dove of peace and plump geese are all favourite Christmas images. The partridge, made popular in the 'The Twelve Days of Christmas', is another favourite. This song is said to have been written during the reign of King Henry VIII of England to remind Catholic children of their doctrine, which they were not allowed to practice openly. The partridge in the pear tree represents Christ on the cross, the two turtle doves, the Old and New Testaments, the three French hens the Trinity or the gifts of the Magi and so on.

Reindeer pulling sleighs and other animals from cold, snowy climates, like the moose, are also common Christmas images, and any other animal can be adapted to fit in with a few appropriate trimmings.

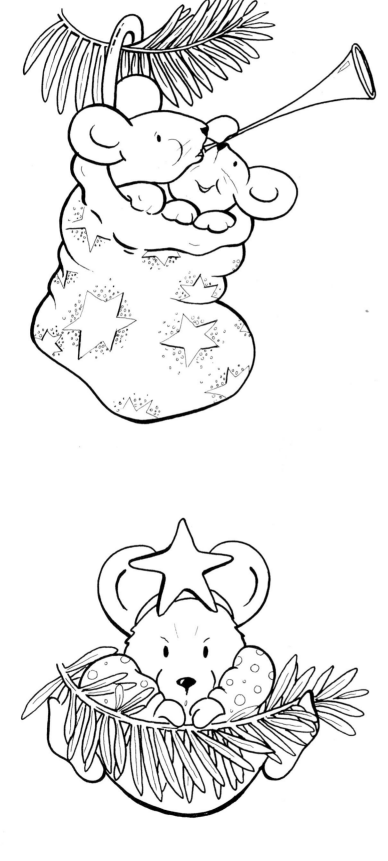

Borders and lettering

Borders, labels, scrolls and fancy lettering are all part of the Christmas tradition because communication is important at this time of year. Seasonal designs can be added to envelopes, cards and banners or used to make simple gift tags.

Borders can range from a simple solid line, to an ornate device featuring familiar festive symbols such as holly, ivy, candles and gifts. They give a wonderful festive feel when applied to a family photograph. Embellished lettering is a simple way to personalize gifts and hand-written messages, and can convey the Christmas message beautifully.

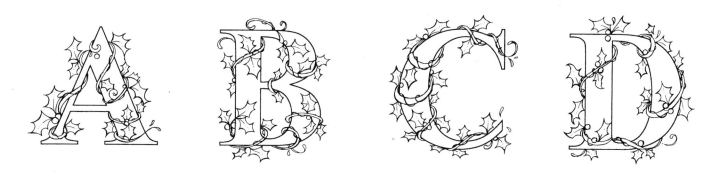

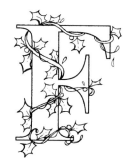

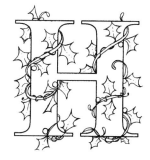

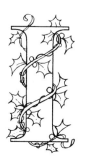

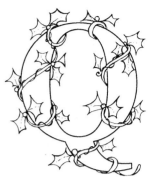

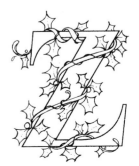

About the author

Sharon Bennett studied graphics and illustration at college before embarking upon a successful career as a packaging designer for various consultancies, eventually becoming Senior Designer for a major confectionery company. In 1989 she became freelance in order to divide her time between her work and bringing up her family. It was during this time that she moved into the craft world and began to contribute projects to national UK magazines such as *Crafts Beautiful*, and worked on their craft booklets. This is her first book. Sharon lives with her family in Halstead, Essex, UK.

Index